# MOON
*In Praise of the Silver Lamp of Night*

# MOON

IN PRAISE OF THE SILVER LAMP OF NIGHT

EDITED BY
*Paula Rees*

HarperSanFrancisco
*An Imprint of* HarperCollins*Publishers*

*Permissions acknowledgments begin on page 84*
*and are a continuation of this copyright page.*

HarperCollins Publishers
1160 Battery Street
San Francisco, CA 94111

FIRST EDITION
Library of Congress Cataloging-in-Publication Data
Moon: In Praise of the Silver Lamp of Night / edited by Paula Rees.—1st ed.
p. cm.
Includes bibliographical references and index.
ISBN 0-06-251260-9 (pbk.: acid-free paper)
1. Moon—Literary collections    I. Rees, Paula.
PN6071.M6M665 1996
808.8'036-dc20        95-43495 CIP
96 97 98 99 00  HAD 10 9 8 7 6 5 4 3 2 1

*What intelligent being, what being capable*

*of responding emotionally to a beautiful sight,*

*can look at the jagged, silvery lunar crescent*

*trembling in the azure sky, even through*

*the weakest of telescopes, and not be struck by it*

*in an intensely pleasurable way,*

*not feel cut off from everyday life*

*here on Earth and transported*

*toward that first step on celestial journeys?*

CAMILLE FLAMMARION

# Contents

# MOON

In a world needing dreams, rest, and certainly more time, the moon reappears as a popular and fitting symbol of the millennium. The passing of round numbered years gives us an affinity with the phasing moon, our closest neighbor. The moon serves as intermediary for questions regarding the physical and heavenly planes. Exquisitely embellished by the stars, the moon's appearance alludes to greater possibilities and provokes questions regarding our very existence.

Whether described as seductress or rock, the moon is more than a counterbalance to our perpetual spinning. Our relationship is not merely gravitational, for the moon is companion to dreamers, and provides enlightenment for the nocturnal. Revealing itself subtly, the moon's task is to softly encourage repose and rejuvenation. Until electricity, the moon was the sole dance partner of firelight. However, in today's artificially bright, twenty-four hour world, we may be kept out of sync with her tides and emanations.

Reflective in character, the moon's personality and profile are simply a mirror of our own position. We can't stare at the sun; our ability to gaze into the uneven face of the moon promotes a better understanding of its distance, and yet a closer familiarity. We become excited when it appears boldly on the horizon. We are repeatedly stunned at its full presentation. For centuries the moon has been the visual marker and timekeeper of the seasons, measuring our labors and signaling agricultural activities with its waxing and waning. In today's hectic world, its cyclic phasing counters our perception of time as a linear event.

Figuratively considered a *she*, the moon has been illustrated throughout history as temptress or Mother Archetype. Endowed with both positive and negative female aspects, the moon is thought shadowy, secretive, absorbing, and fluctuating with mystic influence. Her gift is the color white, pure enough to be described with the vibrancy of silver, in high contrast to a full spectrum of seasonal black-colored skies.

Like a lover, the moon's power seems somehow diminished by our ability to have finally touched it. Is the moon now taken for granted?

In a world of many distractions and an exhaustive pace, *"her influence remains, serene and supreme, a clear mirror rising."*

*Paula Rees*

The Measure
of the Moon

PROVERB

*Pale moon does rain,*

*red moon does bowl:*

*white moon does neither rain nor snow.*

And the light of the moon shall be as the light of the sun.　　　7

ISAIAH 30:26

The Jewish Midrash tells that at the beginning of creation the moon and the sun were of equal size, but that something culpable happened and the moon was diminished while the sun became the ruling heavenly body. God's promise to the moon, however, speaks of the restoration of the original situation in the future:

> In days to come shalt Thou again be great like the Sun; and the Moon's radiance will be as is the radiance of the Sun.

ERICH NEUMANN
*The Moon and Matriarchal Consciousness*

From where I lingered in a lull in March
Outside the sugarhouse one night for choice,
I called the fireman with a careful voice
And bade him leave the pan and stoke the arch:
"O fireman, give the fire another stoke,
And send more sparks up chimney with the smoke."
I thought a few might tangle, as they did,
Among bare maple boughs, and in the rare
Hill atmosphere not cease to glow,
And so be added to the moon up there.
The moon, though slight, was moon enough to show            9
On every tree a bucket with a lid,
And on black ground a bear-skin rug of snow.
The sparks made no attempt to be the moon.
They were content to figure in the trees
As Leo, Orion, and the Pleiades.
And that was what the boughs were full of soon.

ROBERT FROST
*Evening in a Sugar Orchard*

*The moon
also shines,
but does not
warm.*

Let us speak first about the face of the Moon that is turned toward our sight, which, for the sake of easy understanding, I divide into two parts, namely a brighter one and a darker one. The brighter part appears to surround and pervade the entire hemisphere, but the darker part, like some cloud, stains its very face and renders it spotted. Indeed, these darkish and rather large spots are obvious to everyone, and every age has seen them. For this reason we shall call them the large or ancient spots, in contrast with other spots, smaller in size and occurring with such frequency that they besprinkle the entire lunar surface, but especially the brighter part. These were, in fact, observed by no one before us. By oft-repeated observations of them we have been led to the conclusion that we certainly see the surface of the Moon to be not smooth, even, and perfectly spherical, as the great crowd of philosophers have believed about this and other heavenly bodies, but, on the contrary, to be uneven, rough, and crowded with depressions and bulges. And it is like the face of the Earth itself, which is marked here and there with chains of mountains and depths of valleys.

11

GALILEO GALILEI

If the full moon . . . be closely scanned a figure resembling in an extraordinary degree the head of a beautiful woman will be observed. This figure changes its position according as the position of the moon in its orbit varies. For the most part, it will be seen on the extreme right of the moon, with the gaze turned to the left, across the disc, but at times it is in the lower right-hand corner, with the face turned upward. It is a striking apparition, this of the Lady in the Moon, whose beauty captivates the eye at once— especially if the eye be aided with a small opera-glass— as beauty is apt to do. This moon-maiden has found the secret of perpetual youth; she has been young for millions of years. A proud, imperious beauty, with a haughty, almost contemptuous poise of the head. But in the airless moon she remains for ever mute. Though what language could express more than she looks?

JOSEPH H. ELGIE

Treading the soil of the moon, palpating its pebbles, tasting the panic and splendor of the event, feeling in the pit of one's stomach the separation from terra . . . these form the most romantic sensation an explorer has ever known. . . .

> VLADIMIR NABOKOV
> *The New York Times*
> *July 21, 1969*

13

*You can't*

*outrun*

*the moon.*

Who doth not see the measures of the Moon?
Which thirteen times she danceth every year,
And ends her pavan thirteen times as soon
As doth her brother, of whose golden hair          15
She borroweth part and proudly doth it wear.
Then doth she coyly turn her face aside,
That half her cheek is scarce sometimes descried.

      SIR JOHN DAVIES
      *Orchestra*

# A Clear Mirror Rising

*The moon
shines even
in the house
of the outcast.*

Go out of the house to see the moon, and 'tis mere tinsel: it will not please as when its light shines upon your necessary journey.

RALPH WALDO EMERSON

Under my feet the moon
Glides along the river.
Near midnight, a gusty lantern
Shines in the heart of night.
Along the sandbars flocks
Of white egrets roost,
Each one clenched like a fist.
In wake of my barge
The fish leap, cut the water,
And dive and splash.

TU FU
*Brimming Water*

The Autumn night is clear
After the thunderstorm.
Venus glows on the river.
The Milky Way is white as snow.
The dark sky is vast and deep.
The Northern Crown sets in the dusk.
The moon like a clear mirror
Rises from the great void. When it
Has climbed high in the sky, moonlit
Frost glitters on the chrysanthemums.

TU FU
*Stars and Moon on the River*

Slowly, silently, now the moon
Walks the night in her silver shoon;
This way, and that, she peers, and sees
Silver fruit upon silver trees;
One by one the casements catch
Her beams beneath the silvery thatch;
Couched in his kennel, like a log,
With paws of silver sleeps the dog;
From their shadowy cote the white breasts peep
Of doves in a silver-feathered sleep;
A harvest mouse goes scampering by,
With silver claws, and silver eye;
And moveless fish in the water gleam,
By silver reeds in a silver stream.

WALTER DE LA MARE
*Silver*

*Don't love the*

*moon more*

*than the sun.*

I awoke in the Midsummer not to call night,
   in the white and the walk of the morning:
The moon, dwindling and thinned to the fringe
   of a finger-nail held to the candle,
Or paradisaical fruit, lovely in waning but lustreless,
Stepped from the stool, drew back from the barrow,
   of dark Maenefa the mountain;
A cusp still clasped him, a fluke yet fanged him,
   entangled him, not quite utterly.
This was the prized, the desirable sight,
   unsought, presented so easily,
Parted me leaf and leaf, divided me,
   eyelid and eyelid of slumber.

GERARD MANLEY HOPKINS
*Moonrise*

*The full*
*moon*
*eats clouds.*

And who has seen the moon, who has not seen
Her rise from out of the chamber of the deep,
Flushed and grand and naked, as from the chamber
Of finished bridegroom, seen her rise and throw
Confession of delight upon the wave,
Littering the waves with her own superscription
Of bliss, till all her lambent beauty shakes toward us
Spread out and known at last, and we are sure
That beauty is a thing beyond the grave,
That perfect, bright experience never falls
To nothingness, and time will dim the moon
Sooner than our full consummation here
In this odd life will tarnish or pass away.

      D. H. LAWRENCE
      *Moonrise*

27

O lovely moon, I call up in my mind
Now that a year has turned how, full of pain,
I climbed this hill to wonder at your light.
And I beheld you hanging there above
That wood, as now, illuminating all.
But then you shimmered vaguely through the tears
Which brimmed my eyes, for life to me was hard,
And is, nor does it ever seem to change,
My charming moon. And yet, recapturing
And numbering the phases of my grief
Provides a certain balm. How sweet—when we
Are young, when memory is short and hope
Seems endless—the remembrance of things past,
Though they were sad, and though the pain endures.

GIACOMO LEOPARDI
*To the Moon*

*If in the Spring*
*a crescent moon*
*hangs like a cradle,*
*the summer will be dry.*

The harvest moon has no innocence,
like the slim quarter moon of spring twilight,
nor has it the silver penny brilliance of the
moon that looks down upon the resorts of summer time.
Wise, ripe, and portly, like an old Bacchus,
it waxes night after night.

29

DONALD CULROSS PEATTIE
*An Almanac for Moderns*

*Moonlight
does not dry
the malt.*

Watching the moon
at dawn,
solitary, mid-sky,
I knew myself completely:
no part left out.

IZUMI SHIKIBU

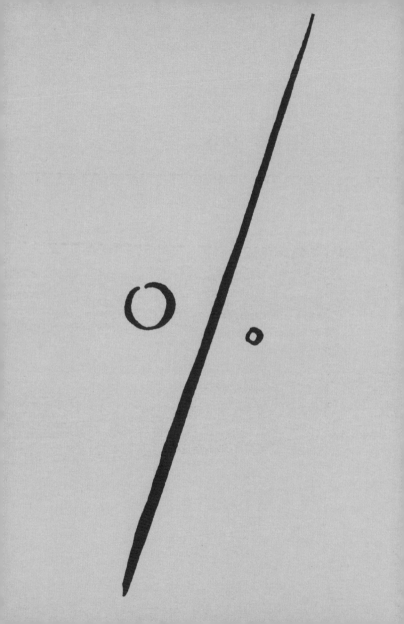

# This Silver Ghost

. . . what barbarian would go bawling
into the night to welcome the moon?
We tread softly; look and think with
caution; as if to be in keeping with
this stealthy and motionless lustre.

35

WALTER DE LA MARE
*Behold This Dreamer!*

*A bright star*
*behind a crescent moon*
*means rain and storm,*
*a star in front or within,*
*means fair.*

In the first of the moon,
All's a scattering,
A shining.

THEODORE ROETHKE
*Meditation at Oyster River*

There is something haunting in the light of the moon;
it has all the dispassionateness of a disembodied soul,
and something of its inconceivable mystery.

JOSEPH CONRAD
*Lord Jim*

Low-hanging moon!
What is that dusky spot in your brown yellow?
O it is the shape, the shape of my mate!
O moon do not keep her from me any longer. . . .


O darkness! O in vain!
O I am very sick and sorrowful.

O brown halo in the sky near the moon, drooping upon the sea!
O troubled reflection in the sea!
O throat! O throbbing heart!
And I singing uselessly, uselessly all the night.

> WALT WHITMAN
> *Out of the Cradle Endlessly Rocking*

Moon, worn thin to the width of a quill,
In the dawn clouds flying,
How good to go, light into light, and still
Giving light, dying.

SARA TEASDALE
*Moon's Ending*

When the full fields begin to smell of sunrise
And the valleys sing in their sleep,
The pilgrim moon pours over the solemn darkness
Her waterfalls of silence,
And then departs, up the long avenue of trees.

THOMAS MERTON
*The Trappist Abbey: Matins*

Tell me, Moon, thou pale and gray
Pilgrim of Heaven's homeless way,
In what depth of night or day
        Seekest thou repose now?

PERCY BYSSHE SHELLEY
*The World's Wanderers*

43

*When round the moon
there is a brugh,
the weather will
be cold and rough.*

Sun of the sleepless! Melancholy star!
Whose tearful beam glows tremulously far,
That show'st the darkness thou canst not dispel,
How like art thou to joy remembered well!
So gleams the past, the light of other days,
Which shines, but warms not with its powerless rays;
A night-beam Sorrow watcheth to behold,
Distinct, but distant—clear, but oh, how cold!

45

LORD BYRON
*Sun of the Sleepless*

Totally conscious, and apropos of nothing, you come to see me.
Is someone here? I ask.
*The moon. The full moon is inside your house.*

My friends and I go running out into the street.
*I'm in here*, comes a voice from the house, but we aren't listening.
We're looking up at the sky.

RUMI
*Be Melting Snow*

| | | |
|---|---|---|
| *Romeo* | Lady, by yonder blessed moon I swear | |
| | That tips with silver all these fruit-tree tops— | |

48    *Juliet*    O! swear not by the moon, the inconstant moon,
That monthly changes in her circle orb,
Lest that thy love prove likewise variable.

WILLIAM SHAKESPEARE
*Romeo and Juliet—II, i*

I would not be the Moon, the sickly thing,
To summon owls and bats upon the wing;
For when the noble Sun is gone away,
She turns his night into a pallid day.

She hath no air, no radiance of her own,
That world unmusical of earth and stone.
She wakes her dim, uncoloured, voiceless hosts,
Ghost of the Sun, herself the sun of ghosts.

The mortal eyes that gaze too long on her
Of Reason's piercing ray defrauded are.
Light in itself doth feed the living brain;
That light, reflected, but makes darkness plain.

MARY COLERIDGE
*In Dispraise of the Moon*

*Let anyone
who despises the
position of the moon
get up and correct it.*

This is the very error of the moon;
She comes more nearer the earth than she was wont
And makes men mad.

51

WILLIAM SHAKESPEARE
*Othello*

# Her Illumination, Silently Disclosing

Only the very timid or guilty *fear* her light, and only the
furtive would shun it. A bad conscience has an assignation
with her; and the earth itself may seem apprehensive of her
unflinching gaze. She can intensify darkness; give magic to
the bewitched; terror to vacancy; horror to the haunted; an
edge to the spectral. Her presence in sky or room deepens
solitude; prepares for the ghostly. And no wonder the tide
of unreason also obeys her influence.

WALTER DE LA MARE
*Behold This Dreamer!*

55

. *The full moon,*

. *brings fair*

. *weather.*

I raise my cup and invite
The moon to come down from the
Sky. I hope she will accept
Me. I raise my cup and ask
The branches, heavy with flowers,
To drink with me. I wish them
Long life and promise never
To pick them. In company
With the moon and the flowers,
I get drunk, and none of us
Ever worries about good
Or bad. How many people
Can comprehend our joy? I
Have wine and moon and flowers.
Who else do I want for drinking companions?

SU TUNG P'O
*Moon, Flowers, Man*

The moon, too, as the heavenly body nearest the earth, bestows her effluence most abundantly upon mundane things, for most of them, animate or inanimate, are sympathetic to her and change in company with her; the rivers increase and diminish their streams with her light, the seas turn their own tides with her rising and setting, and plants and animals in whole or in some part wax and wane with her.

CLAUDIUS PTOLEMY
*Tetrabiblos*

The light and heat of the sun, like air and water, is a human necessity. The moon is in the nature of a luxury. She is sweetheart rather than wife. She is our night-light. The sun excites, challenges, daunts, dazzles, dazes, may even all but stun the mind with radiance. It sucks self outwards; its heat resembles a fourth skin. In its vast shimmering mantle of gold, it pours life into us. . . . Not so the moon. Like a spy with a bull's-eye, she silently discloses what she shines upon. She pacifies, invites us *in*. Her light gnaws away shadow; and glides, smooth and softly as a serpent, from stone on to stone.

59

WALTER DE LA MARE
*Behold This Dreamer!*

The creative process takes place not under
the burning rays of the sun but in the cool,
reflected light of the moon when the darkness
of the unconscious is great: night, not day,
is the time for begetting. Darkness and stillness,
secrecy, remaining mute and veiled, are part of it.
For this reason the moon as lord of life and of
growth is opposed to the death character of the
devouring sun. The nocturnal moistness of the
moon-night is the time of sleep, but also that
of healing and recovery.

ERICH NEUMANN
*The Moon and Matriarchal Consciousness*

The solitary globe of night
pours out its calm and clear light
in the midst of the silence and
contemplation of nature.

CAMILLE FLAMMARION
*Popular Astronomy*

The goddess Night has drawn near, looking about on many
sides with her eyes. She has put on all her glories.
The immortal goddess has filled the wide space, the depths
and the heights. She stems the tide of darkness with her light.
The goddess has drawn near, pushing aside her sister
the twilight. Darkness, too, will give way.
As you came near to us today, we turned homeward to rest,
as birds go to their home in a tree.
People who live in villages have gone home to rest,
and animals with feet, and animals with wings, even the ever-
searching hawks.
Ward off the she-wolf and the wolf; ward off the thief.
O night full of waves, be easy for us to cross over.
Darkness—palpable, black, and painted—has come upon me.
O Dawn, banish it like a debt.
I have driven this hymn to you as the herdsman drives cows.
Choose and accept it, O Night, daughter of the sky,
like a song of praise to a conqueror.

ANONYMOUS VEDIC POET

The moon is a friend for the lonesome to talk to.

CARL SANDBURG
*Moonlight and Maggots*

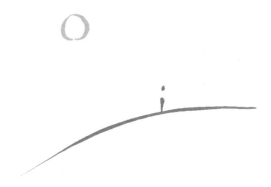

I've tried the new moon tilted in the air
Above a hazy tree-and-farmhouse cluster
As you might try a jewel in your hair.
I've tried it fine with little breadth of luster,
Alone, or in one ornament combining
With one first-water star almost as shining.

I put it shining anywhere I please.
By walking slowly on some evening later
I've pulled it from a crate of crooked trees,
And brought it over glossy water, greater,
And dropped it in, and seen the image wallow,
The color run, all sorts of wonder follow.

ROBERT FROST
*The Freedom of the Moon*

Unlike her lord and master, a Bluebeard who, in her sluggish
rotations, never allows her out of his sight, the moon presides
rather than rules over the earth. . . .

    She pacifies the peaceful—wood, hill and water;
gives wings and a tumultuous sky to the wildest gale; smiles
down from a pale-blue sky of soapsud clouds as benignly as
some old family Nannie on the children of men—
although candour must add that she can be a little dull and
commonplace when gibbous, and rather too sweetly
sentimental on the marine parade. She bestows loveliness
and magic even on the lovely: "How sweet the moonlight
sleeps upon this bank!" She can win back from the darkness
their reds and blues into the flowers, its dyes into the Persian
carpet; can etherealise the ugly; bestow grace on the
commonplace; and will adore her own splintered reflection,
as Tchekhov declared, in every unflattering scrap of broken
crockery or glass.

67

WALTER DE LA MARE
*Behold This Dreamer!*

Art thou pale for weariness
Of climbing heaven and gazing on the earth,
Wandering companionless
Among the stars that have a different birth, —
And ever changing, like a joyless eye
That finds no object worth its constancy?

PERCY BYSSHE SHELLEY
*To the Moon*

At midnight, in the month of June,
I stand beneath the mystic moon.
An opiate vapour, dewy, dim,
Exhales from out her golden rim,
And, softly dripping, drop by drop,
Upon the quiet mountain top,
Steals drowsily and musically
Into the universal valley.

EDGAR ALLAN POE

69

MOON CALENDAR

| | |
|---|---|
| MID-JANUARY | *Full Wolf Moon—* <br> *time to remember the less fortunate* |
| JANUARY 31 | *Chinese Lunar Year Begins* |
| MID-FEBRUARY | *Full Snow Moon* |
| MID-MARCH | *Full Sap Moon* |
| LATE MARCH | *Vernal Equinox begins, the Moon is at perigee—* <br> *the closest approach to Earth* |
| MID-APRIL | *Passover celebrated on second Full Moon* <br> *after Vernal Equinox; full, pink moon and* <br> *small partial eclipse in view in Western U.S.* |
| MID-MAY | *Full Flower Moon* |
| MID-JUNE | *Full Strawberry Moon* <br> *and the earth in conjunction* |

| | |
|---|---|
| MID-JULY | *Full Buck Moon and Neptune in conjunction* |
| MID-AUGUST | *Full Sturgeon Moon* |
| EARLY SEPTEMBER | *The Full Moon is just a bit closer to the equinox than that of the Full Hunter Moon in October— thus earning the title a Harvest Moon* |
| LATE SEPTEMBER | *Autumnal Equinox— Crescent Moon on Equinox* |
| EARLY OCTOBER | *Full Hunter's Moon* |
| EARLY NOVEMBER | *Full Beaver Moon— time to prepare for winter* |
| LATE NOVEMBER | *Thanksgiving, slender Crescent Moon at perigee and joined with Jupiter, Venus, and Mars low in the southwestern sky* |
| EARLY DECEMBER | *Full Cold Moon* |

# Moon Deities

## ALMAQUAH

*Moon-god and tutelary god of the South Arabian kingdom of Saba. Members of the tribe of Saba called themselves "the children of Almaquah." He is symbolized by a cluster of lightning flashes and a weapon that looks like a slightly bent capital S. His symbolic animal is the bull, and in some texts he is referred to as the "Lord of the horned goats."*

## AMM

*The moon-god of pre-Islamic South Arabia. In the kingdom of Qataban he had the status of a tutelary national god, and the people of Qataban called themselves "the children of Amm." His lunar character is indicated by his epithet: "he who waxes."*

## ARMA

*A Hittite moon-god. On reliefs he wears the sickle moon on his pointed and horned cap. On his back he has a pair of wings.*

## ARTEMIS

*The Greek goddess of fertility, and virgin huntress. She was the daughter of Zeus and Leto and the twin sister of Apollo. Graphically, she is depicted as winged and accompanied by lions, deer, and birds. As bearer of light, Phosphorus, she was identified with the moon-goddess Selene. Her Roman equivalent is Diana.*

## AUGHIMALGEN

*Chilean moon-goddess. Caring for mankind she frightened away evil spirits and served as a comfort for the people against their dangerous lifestyles.*

## CANDRA

*The Indian moon-god whose Sanskrit name means "the shining or lovely one." He is white in color and wears white garments, and drives a shining white chariot drawn by ten white horses or antelope.*

## CH'ANG-O

*Chinese goddess of the moon. Drinking her husband's immortal potion of the gods, she fled his anger and lived in a palace on the moon.*

## CHARITIES

*Two Aphrodite-like goddesses of ancient Greece who represent the waxing and waning of the moon.*

COYALXAUHQUI

*Mexican moon-goddess daughter of Mother Earth. She was accidently killed by her brother; he tossed her head up to the sky; golden bells are seen in her cheeks.*

DIANA

*Ancient Roman goddess of the woods and forests, protector of virginity, and worshipped as a moon-goddess. Her name is derived from Diviana, meaning "the shining one." She is equivalent to the Greek goddess Artemis.*

CHONS/KHONS/AAH

*Egyptian moon-god whose name means "he who fares through the heavens." As "Lord of Time" he converges with Thot. He is usually represented as a young man in mummy posture, with his legs close together and a full or crescent moon on his head.*

## GIDJA

*Totemic ancestor and moon-god from the Australian Dreamtime. Responsible for making sex possible.* •

## HECATE

*The Greek guiding goddess of the moon, navigation, magic, and enchantment.*

## HENG E/CHANGE-E

*Chinese goddess of the moon, wife of the sun-god Sheng Yi. She is represented wearing regal garments; in her right hand she carries the disc of the moon. She is the symbolic figure for the female principle yin.*

## HINA/HINE

*In Polynesia, a woman of semi-divine status who appears in the moon; sometimes she is elevated to the rank of moon-goddess. As great goddess of darkness, she appears as the mother or the wife of the culture hero Maui.*

## ILAZKI/ILLARGUI IRETARGUI

*The name given to the moon by Basques; regarded as female and usually known as grandmother or holy grandmother. The name Illargui means "light of the dead," the nocturnal light that shines for the souls of the dead.*

## IXCHEL

*The moon-goddess of the Maya, regarded as the protector of women in childbirth and patron of weavers.*

## JOH

*The Egyptian word for the moon and for the moon-god. Originally much respected especially in Thebes, he was gradually absorbed by Thot.*

## KEMWER

*Sometimes interpreted as the left eye of the moon, often represented as a black bull worshipped in the Egyptian city of Athribis and closely associated with Osiris.*

## KUSUH

*Moon-god of the Hurrians in ancient Asia Minor. His sacred number is 30, corresponding to the lunar month of thirty days.*

## LUNA

*The Roman goddess of the moon equated with the Greek goddess Selene. Her chief temple was on the Aventine Hill, and like the sun-god Sol, was protector of charioteers.*

## MAH

*Persian word for both the moon and moon-god. Mah is the source for the cow, the most important animal in Iranian mythology. Represented on coins in cloak, doublet and trousers, with the tips of the sickle moon sticking out of his shoulders.*

## MANI

*In Northern Germanic tradition the moon or moon-god; the son of Mundiferi, and the brother of Sol, the sun. It is Mani who guides the moon-vehicle through the heavens.*

## MARAMA

*Moon-goddess of the New Zealand Maori. Periodically her body wastes away but is restored to new splendor after bathing in the waters of life.*

## MAWU

*The sky-god of the Ewe people of Togo. He is the giver of all things and loves the color white, even the food he partakes of, is white. Among the Fong people of Dahomey, Mawu is female and is identified with the moon.*

## MEN

*A moon-god honored in Phrygia in Asia Minor, and believed to rule over not only the heavens but also the underworld as well.*

## MENESS

*Old Latvian moon-god, husband of the sun-goddess Saule, and patron god of travelers.*

## MENULIS

*The moon-god of ancient Lithuanians. Called dangaus kar-alaitis, meaning "heavenly prince." He was the husband of the sun, but living apart from her, he came to be in love with the morning star.*

## MYESYATS

*Slavonic young moon maiden of serene beauty, married to the sun-god Dazhbog. Their children are the stars.*

## NANNA/NANNAR

*Sumerian moon-god, whose center was at Ur. The equivalent of Sin, he was regarded as the "lord of destiny," and his epithet was asimbabbar, "whose ascent is radiant."*

## QUILLA

*The moon-goddess of the Inca empire, wife and sister of the sun. Deeply venerated, she was closely associated with the Inca calendar and with all feast days celebrated according to the phases of the moon. She is shown as a silver disc with a human face.*

## PAH

*God of the moon to the Pawnee Indians. Taking his place in the West he gave light to mankind at night. His mate was the Sun-Shakuru.*

## SELENE

*Greek goddess of the moon, daughter of the Titan Hyperion, and sister of the sun-god Helios. She drives a chariot drawn by two horses, or rides a mule. The goddess was regarded as the tutelary deity of magicians and sorcerers. Selene is equivalent to the Roman moon-goddess Luna.*

## PERSE/PERSEIS

*Wife of the Greek sun-god Helios. She embodies the underworld aspect of the moon-goddess. Also known as Neaira, meaning "the new one" or the new moon.*

## SI

*A moon-god heading the pan-
theon worshipped in the ancient
Chimu Empire of Peru. Usually
shown in a sickle moon with a
crown of feathers joined to an
armored backplate.*

## SIN

*The moon-god of the Euphrates-
Tigris region. His symbol is the
sickle moon, which can be con-
strued as a boat; the Babylonian
god himself was called "shining
boat of heaven." Also sometimes
depicted as a bull whose horns are
formed by the sickle of the moon.
Revered as "lord of destiny" and
"god of vegetation." With the
sun-god Samas, he was judge of
heaven and earth. In keeping
with the lunar calendar, he was
associated with the number 30.*

## SOMA

*Hindu moon-god and ambrosia of
immortality and power. The moon
is the cup of Soma.*

## TANIT/TANITH

*Phoenician moon-goddess, symbol-
ized by a circle inside a crescent.*

## TECCIZTECATL

*Wise, old man carrying a shell on
his back; Mexican moon-god.
With butterfly wings, he reaches
the moon's apex.*

## THOT/THOTH

*Ancient Egyptian god of the moon, the calendar, and of chronology. His attribute is writing materials or a palm-leaf. Known as Hermes by the Greeks; inventor of the arts and sciences. As protector of Osiris he came to be seen as a guide and helper of the dead.*

## TSUKI-YOMI

*Japanese moon-god. He arose when the earth-goddess Izanagi washed her right eye in the sea. Called "Moon-Counter," he is associated with the measurement of time and the calendar.*

## XOCHIQUETZAL

*As wife of the Aztec sun-god, she had a lunar character. She was considered the goddess of love, patron of all forms of female handicrafts, and the queen of plants.*

# ACKNOWLEDGMENTS

EPIGRAPH, *Camille Flammarion*, from POPULAR ASTRONOMY, translated by J. Ellard Gore. Published by D. Appleton and Company, New York, 1907.

PAGE 8, *Erich Neumann*, from THE FEAR OF THE FEMININE, translated by Boris Matthews, Esther Doughty, Eugene Rolfe, and Michael Cullingworth. Date of publication 1994. Reprinted with permission of Princeton University Press.

PAGE 9, *Robert Frost*, from THE POETRY OF ROBERT FROST edited by Edward Lathem. Copyright 1936, 1951, © 1956, 1964 by Robert Frost. Copyright © 1964 by Lesley Frost Ballantine. Copyright 1923, 1928 © 1969 by Henry Holt and Company, Inc. Reprinted by permission of Henry Holt and Company, Inc., and Random House UK Ltd.

PAGE 11, *Galileo Galilei*, from SIDEREUS NUNCIUS, translated by Albert Van Helden. Published by the University of Chicago Press. Reprinted by permission of publisher. Copyright © 1980 by the University of Chicago. All rights reserved.

PAGE 12, *Joseph H. Elgie*, from THE STARS, NIGHT BY NIGHT. C. Arthur Pearson Ltd. Published 1916, London.

PAGE 13, *Vladimir Nabokov*, Copyright © 1969 by The New York Times Company. Reprinted by permission.

PAGE 15, *Sir John Davies*, from ORCHESTRA, by Sir John Davies, edited by E. M. W. Tillyard. Acknowledgment to the Estate of E. M. W. Tillyard. Published by Chatto & Windus, 1947.

PAGES 20–21, *Tu Fu*, "*Brimming Water*" and "*Stars and Moon on the River,*" from ONE HUNDRED POEMS FROM THE CHINESE, translated by Kenneth Rexroth. Copyright © 1971 by Kenneth Rexroth. Reprinted by permission of New Directions Publishing Corp.

PAGE 23, *Walter de la Mare*, "*Silver,*" from RHYMES & VERSES: COLLECTED POEMS FOR CHILDREN. Copyright © 1974 by Henry Holt and Company, Inc. Reprinted by permission of The Literary Trustees of Walter de la Mare, and The Society of Authors as their representative.

PAGE 27, *D. H. Lawrence*, "*Moonrise*" by D. H. Lawrence, from THE COMPLETE POEMS OF D. H. LAWRENCE, edited by V. de Sola Pinto & F. W. Roberts. Copyright © 1964, 1971 by Angelo Ravagli and C. M. Weekley, Executors of the Estate of Frieda Lawrence Ravagli and Laurence Pollinger, Ltd. Reprinted by permission of Viking Penguin, a Division of Penguin Books USA, Inc.

PAGE 57, *Su Tung P'o*, "Moon, Flowers, Man," from ONE HUNDRED POEMS FROM THE CHINESE, translated by Kenneth Rexroth. Copyright © 1971 by Kenneth Rexroth. Reprinted by permission of New Directions Publishing Corp.

PAGE 58, *Claudius Ptolemy*, from TETRABIBLOS, edited and translated into English by F. E. Robbins, Ph.D., Cambridge, Mass.: Harvard University Press, 1980. Reprinted by permission of Harvard University Press and the Loeb Classical Library.

PAGE 59, *Walter de la Mare*, from BEHOLD THIS DREAMER!

PAGE 61, *Erich Neumann*, from THE FEAR OF THE FEMININE.

PAGE 62, *Camille Flammarion*, from POPULAR ASTRONOMY.

PAGE 63, *Anonymous Vedic Poet*, "Night," from THE RIG VEDA, selected and translated by Wendy Doniger O'Flaherty. Copyright © 1981 by Wendy Doniger O'Flaherty. Reprinted by permission of Penguin Books, Ltd.

PAGE 64, *Carl Sandburg*, from *Moonlight and Maggots*, THE COMPLETE POEMS OF CARL SANDBURG. Copyright © 1950 by Carl Sandburg and renewed 1978 by Margaret Sandburg, Helga Sandburg Crile, and Janet Sandburg. Reprinted by permission of Harcourt Brace & Company.

PAGE 65, *Robert Frost*, from THE POETRY OF ROBERT FROST.

PAGE 67, *Walter de la Mare*, from BEHOLD THIS DREAMER!

86

PAULA REES *is an environmental designer
residing in Seattle. Her multidisciplinary
design firm,* MAESTRI, *creates and renovates
public spaces internationally. Her background
in design, architecture, world religion, and theater
have lead her to the creation of new symbols and
language which enhance our experience
in both physical and virtual environments.
Rees is a frequent guest speaker and teacher at
universities and design conferences, specializing
in new urban mythologies.*

87

O

DESIGN: *Linda Soukup*
ILLUSTRATION: *Greg Stadler*
SPECIAL THANKS TO:
*Kristin Cammermeyer,
Kelly Brandon & JS*

THIS BOOK WAS TYPESET IN JANSON
FROM THE ADOBE TYPE LIBRARY

*The silent star of night is the first halting-place*

*on a voyage towards the infinite.*

---

CAMILLE FLAMMARION